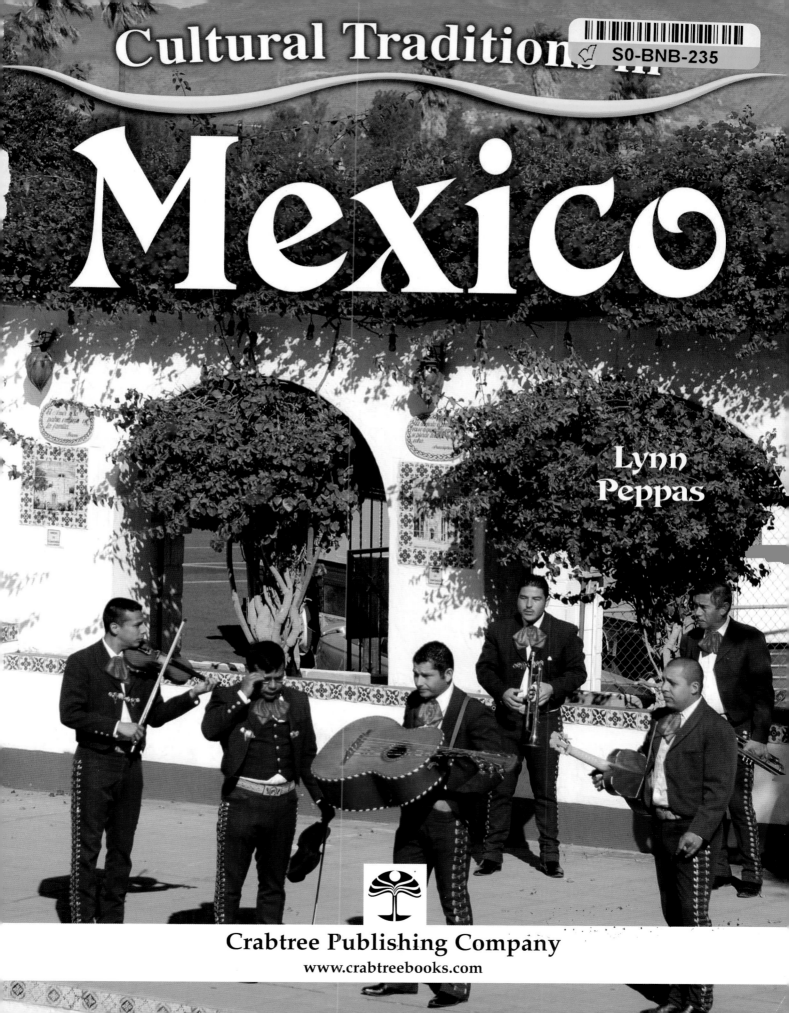

Cultural Traditions in

Mexico

Lynn
Peppas

Crabtree Publishing Company
www.crabtreebooks.com

Crabtree Publishing Company

www.crabtreebooks.com

Author: Lynn Peppas
Publishing plan research and development:
  Sean Charlebois, Reagan Miller
  Crabtree Publishing Company
Project coordinator: Kathy Middleton
Editors: Adrianna Morganelli, Crystal Sikkens
Proofreader: Kathy Middleton
Photo research: Crystal Sikkens
Design: Margaret Amy Salter
Production coordinator: Margaret Amy Salter
Prepress technician: Margaret Amy Salter
Print coordinator: Katherine Berti

Cover: Traditional Mexican piñata (top right and left); Mayan pyramid at Chichen Itza (top center); Mexican children dancing in traditional costumes (middle center); luchador masks used for Mexican wrestling (middle right); salsa fresca (bottom center); Mexican sweet bread and sombrero hats (bottom right); figure from Day of the Dead celebration (bottom left)

Title page: Mexican mariachi band

Illustrations:
Bonna Rouse: page 4

Photographs:
Alamy: © Craig Lovell/Eagle Visions Photography: page 11 (bottom); © Lightworks Media: page 13 (top)
AP Images: Jose Luis Magane: page 20
BigStockPhoto: cover (top right and left)
Dreamstime: © Shootalot: page 5; © Feverpitched: page 8; © Arturo Osorno: page 10; © Ulita: page 18
Keystone Press: © El Universal/Zuma: page 9
Shutterstock: cover (top center, middle right, bottom right and center), pages 6, 13 (bottom), 14; Faraways: cover (middle center); Ron Kacmarcik: page 1; tipograffias: pages 19, 24 (right); Bill Perry: page 27 (right)
Thinkstock: pages 7, 11 (top), 15, 24 (left), 25 (bottom), 26, 27 (left), 29 (left), 30, 31
Wikimedia Commons: Tomascastelazo: cover (bottom left); TheImadatter: pages 16, 17 (top), 22, 28, 29 (right); Luisfi: page 17 (bottom); dbking: page 21; Alejandro Linares Garcia: page 23 (top); Paige Morrison: page 23 (bottom); Eneas de Troya: page 25 (top)

Library and Archives Canada Cataloguing in Publication

Peppas, Lynn
    Cultural traditions in Mexico / Lynn Peppas.

(Cultural traditions in my world)
Includes index.
Issued also in electronic format.
ISBN 978-0-7787-7587-4 (bound).--ISBN 978-0-7787-7594-2 (pbk.)

    1. Festivals--Mexico--Juvenile literature. 2. Holidays--Mexico--Juvenile literature. 3. Mexico--Social life and customs--Juvenile literature. I. Title. II. Series: Cultural traditions in my world

GT4814.A2P47 2012   j394.26972   C2012-900672-6

Library of Congress Cataloging-in-Publication Data

Peppas, Lynn.
    Cultural traditions in Mexico / Lynn Peppas.
        p. cm. -- (Cultural traditions in my world)
    Includes index.
    ISBN 978-0-7787-7587-4 (reinforced library binding : alk. paper) -- ISBN 978-0-7787-7594-2 (pbk. : alk. paper) -- ISBN 978-1-4271-7866-4 (electronic pdf) -- ISBN 978-1-4271-7981-4 (electronic html)
    1. Festivals--Mexico--Juvenile literature. 2. Holidays--Mexico--Juvenile literature. 3. Mexico--Social life and customs--Juvenile literature. I. Title.

GT4814.A2P47 2012
394.26972--dc23
                                              2012003079

Crabtree Publishing Company

www.crabtreebooks.com   1-800-387-7650

Printed in Canada/022012/AV20120110

Published in Canada
Crabtree Publishing
616 Welland Ave.
St. Catharines, ON
L2M 5V6

Published in the United States
Crabtree Publishing
PMB 59051
350 Fifth Avenue, 59th Floor
New York, New York 10118

Published in the United Kingdom
Crabtree Publishing
Maritime House
Basin Road North, Hove
BN41 1WR

Published in Australia
Crabtree Publishing
3 Charles Street
Coburg North
VIC 3058

Contents

Welcome to Mexico

Mexican culture is a unique mixture of Native Mexican and Spanish traditions. Culture is a group of people's shared history and beliefs. Traditions are ways that people celebrate their culture that are passed down to others. Thousands of years ago Mexico was ruled by powerful ancient cultures—mainly the Aztecs and the Mayans. In the 1500s Spanish explorers came to Mexico to claim new lands for Spain. They **conquered** the Native Mexicans and brought their own culture, religion, and traditions with them.

Hernán Cortés was the first Spanish explorer to meet the Aztecs. The first meeting was friendly, but later Cortés and his army conquered the Native Mexicans.

Holidays in Mexico are special days that celebrate the different traditions that have been passed down for hundreds of years. Some holidays are **national** celebrations when most people get the day off work or school. Some of these holidays are **religious** celebrations such as Easter or Christmas. Some celebrations are family occasions such as birthdays, name days, and Mother's Day.

Did You Know?
Fiesta means feast day or party in Spanish. Many Mexican celebrations include fiestas.

Birthdays and Weddings

Mexican families get together to celebrate special occasions such as weddings, anniversaries, and birthdays. A piñata is a fun toy used to celebrate occasions such as birthdays. It is made of glued pieces of paper and is hollow inside. It is stuffed with small presents such as candies, toys, and coins. During a party, a blindfold is placed over children's eyes.

They try to break it open with a wooden stick. Everyone rushes forward to get the goodies when it breaks!

Did You Know?
In Mexico, a girl's 15th birthday is a special celebration called Quinceañera. Young girls usually wear a white dress to mark the occasion.

During wedding ceremonies in Mexico, a rope called a lasso is loosely tied in a figure eight around the necks of the bride and groom. The lasso is made from ribbon, **rosary beads**, or flowers. This shows they are now married and joined together. The groom gives the bride 13 gold coins called arras. The 13 coins represent Jesus and his 12 apostles, or Jesus' followers.

Arras is a Spanish word that means **dowry**.

Family Days

Mothers get special treatment on Mother's Day.

Family life plays an important role in Mexican culture. Mexicans celebrate different members of the family at different dates during the year. Mother's Day is celebrated on May 10. Many serenade, or sing to, their moms or even hire mariachi bands. Mariachi is a traditional music played with guitars, violins, and trumpets.

Children's Day is celebrated on April 30. Children get the day off from school. They are made to feel special and are often given a gift from a parent or caregiver. Some organizations gather donations for orphans or needy children who do not have a lot.

Did You Know?
Father's Day in Mexico is celebrated on the third Sunday in June. Family Day in Mexico falls on the first Sunday in March. And don't forget the grandparents–their day is on August 28.

Children line the streets in Mexico City for a parade on Children's Day.

Name Day and Saints' Day

Most Mexicans follow the Roman Catholic religion. Many Mexicans are named after Catholic **saints**. On the day of a saint's birthday, those named after the saint celebrate too. It is called their "name day." Mexicans often go to church on this day.

In Chiapa de Corzo, Chiapas, Mexico, traditional dancers called Parachicos dance in the street during the Great Feast Festivity to honor their **patron** saints—Our Lord of Esquipulas, Saint Anthony Abbot, and Saint Sebastian.

Different towns and cities in Mexico have a special patron saint that they honor. On the saint's birthday the whole city or town celebrates with a fiesta or festival. A statue of the saint is often paraded through the city. People celebrate the day with music, dancing, and fireworks.

Did You Know?
Sometimes Mexicans pray to their patron saints to ask for special help.

To celebrate the patron saint of San Miguel de Allende, a statue of San Miguel Arcangel is paraded through the streets.

New Year's Day

New Year's Day is called *Año Nuevo* in Spanish. It is celebrated on January 1, as it is in many other countries, such as the United States and Canada. It is a public holiday, and most people get the day off school or work.

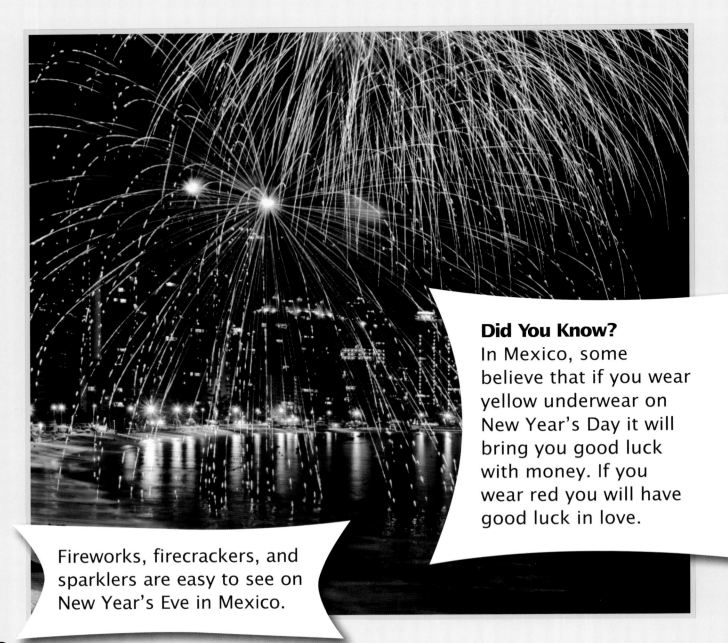

Did You Know?
In Mexico, some believe that if you wear yellow underwear on New Year's Day it will bring you good luck with money. If you wear red you will have good luck in love.

Fireworks, firecrackers, and sparklers are easy to see on New Year's Eve in Mexico.

Mexican sweet bread (right) is a delicious New Year's treat in Mexico. A coin is baked into the bread that will be eaten during the fiesta on New Year's Day. The lucky person who finds the coin during the fiesta will have good luck in the coming year.

(above) Many people have a late night dinner on New Year's Eve. At the stroke of midnight everyone eats 12 grapes and makes a wish for the new year after each grape.

Birthday of Benito Juarez

Many Mexicans believe Benito Juarez was the greatest president that Mexico ever had. Juarez was the president of Mexico in the late 1800s. He was the first indigenous president of Mexico. Indigenous means a person is native to the area. Benito Juarez's birthday is on March 21. The holiday used to be celebrated on this day.

Many monuments and statues of Benito Juarez were erected throughout Mexico honoring the president.

The Mexican 20 pesos bill has Benito Juarez on it.

Mexicans celebrate the birthday of Benito Juarez (*Natalicio de Benito Juarez*) on the third Monday in March. It is a national holiday in Mexico. A national holiday is a special day when almost all Mexicans get the day off of work and school. National holidays celebrate the **history** of a country.

15

Carnival

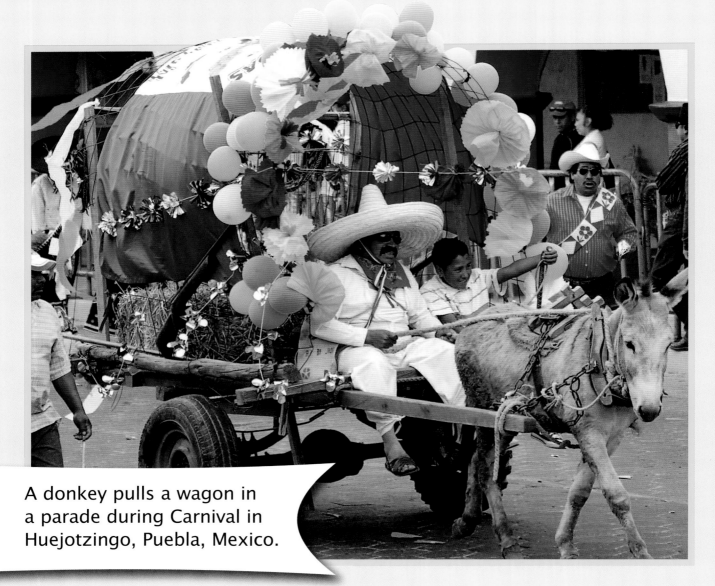

A donkey pulls a wagon in a parade during Carnival in Huejotzingo, Puebla, Mexico.

Carnival is a five-day festive holiday in Mexico. It is celebrated just before Lent begins. Lent is a time when **Christians** give up something they enjoy for 40 days before Easter. Carnival is held on different dates every year. It is usually held sometime in the month of February, depending on when Easter is.

Music is a big part of Carnival, too.

Carnival is a happy time when Mexicans enjoy eating rich food and having parties before the more serious Easter holiday begins. Parades take place in big cities with floats and people in costume. People throw confetti at the floats. As part of the fun, a Carnival Queen and King are crowned.

Did You Know?
Mexicans break cascarones (below) over one another during Carnival. Cascarones are eggshells that have been emptied and refilled with confetti.

Easter

Easter is a religious holiday that is celebrated by Christians all around the world. At Easter, Christians give thanks that Jesus Christ came back to life and went to heaven after being killed. In Mexico, Easter is a very important, two-week holiday. It falls on different days during March or April from year to year. Most Mexicans get this time off from work and school.

Some Mexican villages hold resurrection dances on Easter Sunday to celebrate Jesus's rise to heaven.

Actors are shown recreating the life and death of Jesus during the Easter holiday in Tlalnepantla, Mexico.

Easter is a serious time when Mexicans go to church. Many watch passion plays. Passion plays are performances with actors in costume. They act out the last days of Jesus's life.

Cinco de Mayo

Cinco de Mayo is a holiday held on May 5. *Cinco de Mayo* means May 5 in Spanish. It marks an important time in Mexico's history. About 150 years ago, France tried to invade Mexico. On May 5, the Mexican army drove the French army back in the Battle of Puebla. On this day, Mexicans celebrate their freedom and culture.

On Cinco de Mayo in Puebla, Mexico, actors reenact the battle that took place there in 1862 when the Mexican army defeated the French army.

Many Mexicans celebrate Cinco de Mayo, especially in areas of Mexico such as the state of Puebla. The day is usually spent learning about Mexican culture from art shows or speeches. Many people in the southern United States celebrate the day with Mexican music, food, and dancing.

Many people of Mexican heritage live in the United States. They celebrate Cinco de Mayo too! These dancers are part of a celebration in Washington, DC.

Did You Know?
The first Cinco de Mayo celebration was held in the American state of California!

Mexican Independence Day

The president of Mexico makes a special speech on September 15 to begin the festivities for Mexican Independence Day.

Mexican Independence Day is a **patriotic**, national holiday celebrated every year on September 16. Independence means a group of people are able to make and follow their own rules. On September 15, at 11 p.m., millions of Mexicans watch the president of Mexico make a patriotic speech. The next day is filled with **military** parades and fiestas throughout Mexico.

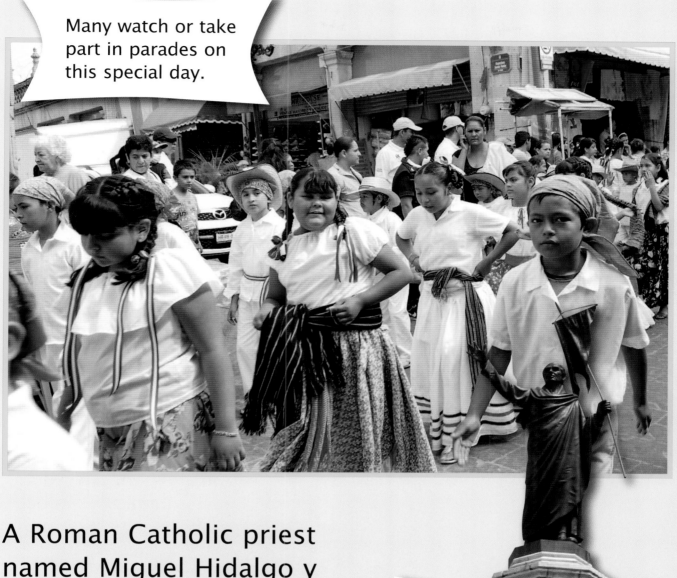

Many watch or take part in parades on this special day.

A Roman Catholic priest named Miguel Hidalgo y Costilla began the Mexican War of Independence on September 16, over 200 years ago. He told the Mexican people to fight against the Spanish who ruled over them. It took over 10 years of war before Mexicans won their independence.

Did You Know?
Sometimes Mexican Independence Day is called the Cry of Dolores (*Grito de Dolores*). That is because Father Hidalgo talked the Mexican people into fighting from the Mexican city of Dolores.

Day of the Dead

Day of the Dead is an ancient holiday that is celebrated on November 1 and 2. Ancient Aztecs were the first to honor their relatives who had died. Later, the Spanish brought their religious holidays that honored the dead to Mexico. Today, Day of the Dead is a tradition blended from both cultures.

Skeleton decorations help celebrate Day of the Dead in Mexico.

On Day of the Dead, many families visit and decorate graveyards where relatives are buried.

Day of the Dead is a happy time when Mexicans celebrate the lives of relatives or friends who have died. Graveyards and homes are decorated with flowers and skeletons. Some believe that the dead return to visit them during this festive time. Families get together for picnics at graveyards to make the spirits of the dead feel welcome.

Did You Know?
Day of the Dead foods include candies that are skeleton shaped, and a special coffee cake called Bread of the Dead.

Day of Our Lady Guadalupe

Day of Our Lady Guadalupe is celebrated in Mexico on December 12. It is Mexico's most important religious holiday. Lady Guadalupe is Jesus's mother, Mary. She is sometimes called the Virgin Mary, or the Virgin of Guadalupe. Hundreds of years ago, a Native Mexican named Juan Diego said the Virgin Mary's spirit had visited him. She performed a miracle by turning a cactus bush into a rose bush and asked to have a church built in Mexico City in her name.

This statue, showing the Virgin Mary appearing to Juan Diego, is located at one of the spots where Juan Diego is said to have seen her.

Today many Mexicans visit the chapel that was built for the Virgin of Guadalupe. Others go to their own churches and pray to the Lady Guadalupe. People celebrate with fiestas and different Mexican foods. Children dress up in, a traditional cloak called a *tilma* like Juan Diego had worn.

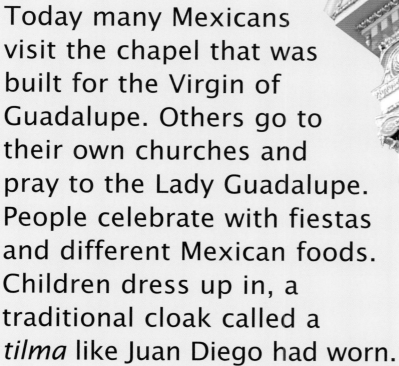

Did You Know?
Mexicans honor the Lady of Guadalupe with statues and pictures in their homes and businesses all year round. She is the patron saint of Mexico.

This woman is praying to the Lady Guadalupe at a church in Mexico City.

Christmas in Mexico

Christians around the world celebrate Christmas on December 25. Jesus Christ was born on this day in the city of Bethlehem. Christmas in Mexico is called *Navidad*, which is Spanish for Christmas. In Mexico the celebration lasts for up to two weeks. Most Mexicans get Christmas Day off from school or work but many families take longer vacations at this time. At Christmas, many Mexicans go to church.

Many markets sell handmade Christmas decorations, such as this one in Michoacan, Mexico.

On Christmas Eve they go visit friends and family asking for a place to stay just as Mary and Joseph did over 2,000 years ago. At one house they will be invited in and a well-planned fiesta begins. One traditional food served is *Ensalada de Noche Buena*, a Christmas Eve salad.

Families gather in beautifully decorated churches at Christmas.

Did You Know?
Children in Mexico do not get Christmas gifts until January 6—the day the three Wise Men brought gifts to baby Jesus.

Tamales are ground meat wrapped in dough. This popular dish was first introduced by the Spanish to Mexico hundreds of years ago.

Day of the Innocents

Day of the Innocents is celebrated on December 28 in Mexico. This tradition was brought over from Spain hundreds of years ago. It is much like April Fools' Day in North America. In Mexico people play pranks on others or try to trick them into believing something that is not true. When someone falls for their trick they say "*Inocente palomita.*" This is Spanish for "innocent little dove."

Did You Know?
In Mexico people do not lend money to others on Day of the Innocents. The tradition is that any money borrowed on this day does not have to be paid back!

Day of the Innocents is not a religious holiday, but it does have a religious history. Long ago when Jesus was born, an ancient king had heard that a baby named Jesus would grow up and replace him as king. He did not know where Jesus was, so he ordered that all young boys in the town of Bethlehem be killed. Many innocent children died. The king sent the three Wise Men to find Jesus, but when they found him, they did not tell the king where he was. The king was angry at being tricked by the Wise Men.

Glossary

Christian A person who believes that Jesus Christ is the Son of God

conquer To take over by force

dowry A gift given during a marriage

history Events that have happened during the past

military A country's armed forces

national Belonging to a country

patriotic To feel love for one's country

patron Someone who protects, or supports, another

religion A person's belief in God

rosary beads A prayer necklace made of beads

saint A holy person who has died and is believed to have special powers to help others still on Earth

Index